INCONTINENCE

Phoenix Poets

A SERIES EDITED BY ROBERT VON HALLBERG

SUSAN HAHN

Incontinence

THE UNIVERSITY OF CHICAGO PRESS

Chicago and London

SUSAN HAHN is coeditor of *TriQuarterly* and coeditor of
TriQuarterly Books. Her poems have appeared in journals such as
Atlantic Monthly, Kenyon Review, North American Review, Poetry,
and *Virginia Quarterly Review*. The University of Chicago Press
also published her first book of poetry, *Harriet Rubin's Mother's
Wooden Hand*.

The University of Chicago Press, Chicago 60637
The University of Chicago Press, Ltd., London
© 1993 by The University of Chicago
All rights reserved. Published 1993
Printed in the United States of America
02 01 00 99 98 97 96 95 94 93   1 2 3 4 5

ISBN: 0-226-31271-2 (cloth)   0-226-31272-0 (paper)

Library of Congress Cataloging-in-Publication Data

Hahn, Susan.
        Incontinence / Susan Hahn.
            p. cm. —(Phoenix poets)
        I. Title. II. Series.
        PS3558.A323815 1993
        811'.54—dc20   92-10071
                                CIP

♾ The paper used in this publication meets the minimum requirements of the
American National Standard for Information Sciences—Permanence of Paper
for Printed Library Materials, ANSI Z39.48-1984.

For Frederic L.
For Frederic F.

For Jessie and Sol

Why didst thou promise such a beauteous day,
And make me travel forth without my cloak...

William Shakespeare Sonnet xxxiv

Contents

Acknowledgments

Grateful acknowledgment is made to the editors of the publications in which these poems, or versions of them, first appeared:

The Atlantic Monthly "Heart"
Boulevard "Jealousy," "Obsession"
The Kenyon Review "Susan Hahn"; New Series, Fall 1992, vol. 14, no. 4, copyright 1992 by Kenyon College
Michigan Quarterly Review "Itch," "Virgin"; courtesy of the *Michigan Quarterly Review*
The North American Review "Briefcase"
Pequod "Devices for Torture," "The Hope," "The Shape of Happiness," "Rejection," "Rib"
Poetry "Between Rosh Hashanah and Yom Kippur," "Calendar," "The Hemlock Society," "Incontinence," "Oral Interpretation"
Poetry East "Dialysis," "Directions to Where I Live," "Sex Primer, circa 1960"
Prairie Schooner "Half Price," "Mania"; reprinted from *Prairie Schooner* by permission of University of Nebraska Press © 1993 University of Nebraska Press
River Styx "Nerve"
Shenandoah "Hysterectomy as Metaphor"; reprinted from *Shenandoah:* The Washington and Lee University Review with the permission of the editor

The Virginia Quarterly Review "Bone," "Transplant"

"Incontinence," "Jealousy," "Mania," "Masochism," "Obsession,"
and "Suicide" also appeared in the chapbook *Melancholia,
etcetera,* David Sellers, editor, Pied Oxen Printers, Hopewell,
New Jersey, 1993.

INCONTINENCE

Virgin

Before the trespass
of ink no eraser can scratch out,
before the race to command
impossible stanzas and the dream
of rhythms that can't be held
and the ache from the wait between
the times the scheme fits
perfectly, before you and I

and any knowledge
that we would ever be
read about, page and pen
were at peace; before
the arrow arched
into the bull's-eye of the unspoiled
place, this sweet tissue
remained unmarked.

Princess

Your hair, strong and long, longer
than any other woman's in the neighborhood—
Grandmother, years in the grave, gone
mad because you lost him, lost
yourself in the new country with too many
children who couldn't understand the parting

of hair—how you needed him to caress
the strands up and into your very skin.
He was so young when he died and left you

with all that hair—
mane of a thoroughbred—never going
gray as you went from crazy
to crazier, its sheen refusing
to dull even as you snarled
it, tried to make it look
like your wrecked mind
and the nurses, the kindest ones, always
brushing out the tangles,

calling to you, *Rapunzel,*
believing you heard them,
but what you really heard was
him. And how the color would rise
in you and your hair
hung long as you longed for him
and O how it kept as it was then.

II

It was my stubborn hair I'm sure,
how it was like yours, that pulled me
down and through this twisted journey.
How I messed with my crown,
asked each passerby to kiss it, crack it—
bought a brush with a tortoise handle
and the hardest bristles so I could feel
a rush and twinge
I didn't understand. My head-

dress still holds as I travel slowly
to old age and a hundred
shrinks cannot wash out
its shine, comprehend the intricate
wind of its legacy. As you nap

under the granite someone ascends
my hair, as he did yours, and
my angelic love rubs it to its roots
until his arm grows numb
and my mind goes dumb.

Directions to Where I Live

Pass the fragile hepatica and wild
geraniums that trim the tollway,
exit at Willow and travel east
against the sun on its excitable
noonday rise, ride with caution
five miles to the street cordoned off
the day they couldn't stop
the crazy girl from shooting
six children in school.
Where the road ends, turn west
for about a block, then north to Scott.
It's second on the left,
facing south, with the heart-
shaped blossoms dangling
on delicate arched stems
tangled below the windows—
a sheltered locale. Enter my house
as if it were my body,
with gentle eyes, trustworthy smile.

A Waiting Like This

She feels she's caught inside
a container with tiny
holes punched into its lid
and breathes hard,
fantasizes how easily
her cramped neck will curve
around his in the spring
air, in the storybook
garden where only they create
the seconds. Seven days become
eternity after the suspended
years. She's never known

a waiting like this.
The TV's on or the radio—the world
whips by with all its words,
so jarring to the woman
who silenced hers—lips always
quivering. Now she practices opening
them wide in front of her mirror, wishes
the six tomorrows and their sluglike nights
would catapult themselves into the moment
when she's able to unlatch the door,
see him. She's frightened
she's held back too long
with the click and inch

of the clock—the only sound
she focuses on except
for her own *bless you, bless you*
like after a sneeze—a plea
for safekeeping against the kick
and halt of all covetous small-minded gods.

Dialysis

You guide me to your wrist,
where they made the artery and vein
connect. The lush beat
that is your heart rushes
through my fingertips. I lift
it to my ear and hear the echo
of oceans—the second day of creation.
You show me how you placed
the needles in your arm
three days a week for sixteen years—
attached yourself to that miracle
machine. The blood swirls
through my body and comes around
so clean. Love

becomes fresh again, dances
through our hands—jitterbugs,
then waltzes. You hold me
as if we could remain
like this forever, redeemed
like the moment when they joined
your artery to your vein,
artery to vein.

Transplant

Your scar is like a trumpet vine
and by day I am the full sun
pouring over it. At night
I am the eager moon
drawing you up and toward me.
The fragrance you carried with you

in a sachet in your pocket from Hawaii
stays next to me in my writing
room, close to my pen and sweet
yellow paper. It covers the time I have
between hearing your voice
on the phone or at the door,
it nurtures as the pills you swallow
after each meal keep the kidney
well. Life is all

we talk about. I never ask
how long it will last or do you
know who gave you this gift,
but I see a soul sparkling
in the dark among the stars
and feel the merging of paths,
the strength of the ways
we are all attached.

His Shoes

Tonight my husband's shoes lie vacant
on the floor while you fill
the cathedral I make
with my hands—one of yours inside
mine. The little temple
walls I build with my palms
hold your impatient fingers
as you move me and I allow
their rhythm to run
through my limbs.
Tomorrow he'll put his shoes on,
rush across the ground
that readies itself

for snowdrops and crocuses.
And by the time of daffodils
you'll be seeping
from the most precious part
of my heart. A narrowing
will form and a crust I can feel
even now that begins to cling
to words we say and do not
trust. Spring will come

home full bloom and my husband
arrive each evening—his shoes
brushing by lily-flowered
tulips and allium. He'll dust
the early summer air,
already old and swollen
with mold and pollen.

This Autumn

The leaves singed with orange
on the tree outside my door
remind me of my hands
when they touch yours, the heat
in my fingertips, how they burn
into your palms. My body has begun

to snarl like the branch
I see through the pane that tries
to twist away from winter
and this is why I run
to see you again—to reverse
the hardness in our voices,
forget the cold that is on me,
how the joint flames
in my thumb, nags against my pen.
I know the whole of me will stiffen and bend,

but not this season when I still rush
to be lifted into your warm limbs,
block out all the harsh
words that are between us.
For now, I will
not give in to the wind.

Night of the Blue Moon

Naked, bursting bright she appears
twice in the same month, hovers
over her darling, blind

to his imperfections. He takes
delight in her loving shape as she orbits
him, but she knows flushed
as he is, it's never enough for her
to hold him, though tonight she'll hope

until she feels his eventual pull away.
Daybreak she'll leave, vow not to expose
her full gleam as frequently,
recover from this grief that needs
almost a thousand nights to sift through.
Then she'll try again, surprise him

with an extra arrival, reveal
her ripe ecstatic light and pray
he'll beg her to return more often
or better yet to stay.

Bone

I wait for one more call,
your voice soft as the marrow
I'd push my tongue into
then suck and swallow
as a child. Tomorrow I'll hope

for an envelope fat with love
or on this autumn evening
when the paper birch outside my window shines
yellow and the staghorn sumac orange to red—
its berries clumped like excitable clots—
that the phone, white as bone licked vulture
clean, will ring. I crave this magic
as I did from the dead animal

on our table when I was little,
reaching deep into its carcass
for the fragile shape
of happiness—the snap of being
able to say *it's mine,*
I can have this wish.

Rib

At 2 A.M. when drink uncoils
kinked nerves and words slither,
you call to say
I Love You and it's hard
to have sex sometimes
without passion, but she lets you in
for dinner and you use her
piano to practice "Rhapsody
in Blue" and all of this is better
than going home empty and alone.
I listen to how

the kidney's doing well and you piss
frequently, especially at night.

I don't tell what I feel—
about my heart, how it isn't
beating right, the gag
that any woman could
have been created from the rib
of man, that your body's
parts have stopped
adding up to human
and how in the raven hole

of this phone after two hours of chatter
I'm so finally detached
from your voice and more,
disconnected from all matter.

Double Star

I follow you through the winter night sky
to a thousand miles from here
and watch you kiss her with a kiss
that comes less from desire,
more from loneliness—
good enough for the short life
that has to make no promise.
I witness as you place yourself
inside her small space

and when finished detach and drift away
onto the pillow, look above
the crust of snow that almost coats the window—
my hot eyes there to try to pull
you back to last

summer when we were closer
than we've ever been to the fiery
heavens, luminous in perfect orbit.

February Red

I thumb through the *I Love You*'s
to buy some for my husband and son,
men who've seen me at my worst—ragged
with the moon-held spasms, swollen
in the messy crimson of grief over the death
of a friend or what I've seen on TV, soaked in
tears of fruitless rage when I try to comprehend
the ruby sun and its ultimate abandonment
of us. For whatever reasons,

they think well of me, I know,
and tomorrow will show it
with rosy cards carefully chosen,
not unlike the ones I fondle
and wish to send into the indifferent
night sky where everything is drifting

apart. I want to find the exact lines
to pull our universe back.
How I need to reach you.
But too much overheated blood clogs

this tiny shop, scarlet with decorations
and parched air—the odor of heavy winter
coats, red bleeding hearts.

The Cold Hands of the Widow's Husband

You tell me the joke her husband
told two days before he died,
describe how you laughed
together, man to man,
and how you took his icy hands
and asked if you could warm them
in the racy heat

of yours. Now that he's gone
they freeze and thaw
under the ambivalent April soil,
their fingernails growing as they mime
the snow crocus, while you watch
his widow weep in the sweet smell
of her kitchen, offer her
hot tea and hugs—
the nourishment of loss and love.
You massage the quiver

in your own thinned bones
and whisper to me
I helped her pick the casket,
she didn't buy a double
headstone, forty is too young
to decide who one should lie next to
for eternity. All the time I know

soon you'll dream of her
hands, their sultry manicure of red,
and wait for the swelter of midsummer
when you'll finally let go
of the feel of his fragile wrist,
its shiver as you circled it
in the frigid heat of his late winter bed.

The Real Laws of Motion

Tonight you bite the widow's
nipples, stick your forefinger between
her lips and wish she'll know
to suck it, then understand
to move herself down
below the trellis scar,
where you hold the hope some life
still exists. Her husband six weeks
in his casket and I on the flaccid
ground feel the twist
of the two of you against her just-washed
sheets. Everything's so fresh:
death, the oozing crust that surrounds
my heart, your touch
to her excited breasts.

Do I wish you happiness, and her?
I guess.

She tended him for two long years
and you've carried your own grief
for twenty, deep inside your belly
and in a vial of pills meticulously
filled and kept vest close.
But the midnights when
the phone rings and it is

or is not you, I knot
into such sadness as I remember
you perfect, with your smile
at sixteen, the boy across the aisle,
the first week of physics class,
years before I learned
the real laws of motion—
the power of the atmosphere,
its tug on all we love.

Sex Primer, circa 1960

It was so dirty
I didn't want to touch it—
the untitled cover, a slack,
gray cloth, spotted
from the many adolescent
hands that had played with it.
It came from the Levy family:
the parents always bickering
with each other and five wild kids
who must have slammed it
against walls, laughed
at the flying pages filled
with print and sketches
of horses, pigs, and dogs.
No human was drawn.

My mother brought it to me
while I daydreamed in bed
listening to Johnny Mathis sing
"A Certain Smile" on the radio.
Her fingers shivered
as she pulled it from her
apron pocket, made the presentation
with the words *please*
ask if you have any questions.
But I'd already begun

to tuck them within myself
and placed the book
deep on a closet shelf,
used Kleenex the few times
I gingerly thumbed through, wishing
it'd been clean and new—
lustrous, like the lyrics
crooned into my room.

Obsession

Somewhere while another woman spreads
herself below the summer sky and you
fly into her over and over,
I am the empty space, the blank

on your machine,
noting how long you hold on to
the vowels, especially the "O's"—
those secure, never-ending
circles. Again and again I listen
to your recorded *Hello,*
while outside the healthy sounds

of July glide by and in the fertile ground
the impatiens multiply.
(I don't know how many
times I'll try your number
this hour.) It's almost too hot to be
inside the way my blood rises and floods
my flesh. How smooth and perfect

she must be from your constant
rub, like the pebbles on the beach you share.
Here, an expanse of ocean is only a dream,
the lightning hits without warning
and the hard sudden rain frightens like shots
on TV or up the block. *Hands up,*

I promise for the minute not to touch
the phone—the only weapon this victim
has for not feeling so alone.

The Center

Two days in the Poconos
with you in a heart-
shaped tub blowing the scented
bubbles below the water level,
holding her body down the way
her husband didn't
the last year when he could barely
bow himself out
of his sweat-soaked bed,
how vulnerable she is—
so tired of lying against
the cold and wet
that she lets you in to heat her,
kiss after kiss—your fish lips
not needing to come up
for breath until you please her
silent wish. Here the music

on the radio longs for love
lost, while I toss in what was once
our tangled bed, my just washed hair
not clean enough, and caress
the tuft in the center
of my head, searching for the lotus
and a peace that goes beyond the flesh.

Rejection

My heart has nothing
to do with it, it still hopes
in hops and leaps to the beat
of your voice, forgives the shallow
and the deep betrayals while your body
slowly shows the signs it doesn't want

the cadaver's gift and you tell me
of the fever and the bloat,
how your blood count is all
wrong and in the kitchen
some new woman is stirring
soup, ready to ladle it to
your lips and if it pleases,
into your mouth for a gulp.
Soon surgeons will syphon the fluid

from the worn-out
kidney that's already been part of one
death—that body long buried and visited
sometimes by someone with flowers.
Tonight, the cemetery's only color is dust
from the crush of autumn
leaves. From my room

I stare at the stubborn one that still cleaves
to the fossil ginkgo tree as we talk across
the wind-twisted miles and I imagine
the other woman, her moist
hands brewing the elixir
she believes will make you love her
and you so eager to swallow her juice,
as if it were the cure.

Jealousy

She sings *Hello* with a hold
on the *lo* as if it were part of a lullaby
and children were happily napping
around her, so safe in

her voice, while I smother
my breath and hope for anger
when I say nothing back—
lips bitten to cracked.
No matter how many times
I call her sweet mood

won't change as my spine twists
and discs lurch out of place.
Over and over I split

my nails as I punch
her number and she is there, lenient
mother against my sunken silence.

Last Love Songs

Your polite message
saying you're not there,
the carol of it is warmer
than any real *Hello*—
your melody to me as flat
as my imprint in the hard shallow
January snow. How cold your insides
grow with passion thin as the scratch
of twigs against my frozen window—
biting and impossible
as the forecast for more

wind and sleet and war.
So I gather your heated notes
into an envelope I'll send
to some distant part
of my room while somewhere
men and women sweat

under a fat furious sun
and write their love songs
home until the bullet hits
and somewhere that paper
will be all that's left
to hold on to—recordings

blared into the bony labyrinth
of the ear like a riot
until it becomes background hum.

The Shape of Happiness

The pharmacist hands her a vial
filled with cream/green capsules
and she places them in the wide smile
of her open purse. Hopefully,
she takes them home to swallow
one by one, day by day, and prays
they'll make the world
seem brighter than the slush

she's been pushing through all March.
This winter she's seen pictures on TV
of gangsters' houses in Key Biscayne
and there are times she wants so much to live
in a walled-in, protected place,
without pain, next to dazzling water
where the evil is buried so deep
under each foundation that the beautiful women
who float above never think to see
it, their frontal lobes deadened
or so she imagines, as she accepts
the small bullet shape into her mouth
and waits for it to target
the right place in her brain.
Then, she won't care

that he's forgotten. Who she was
has become a memory
even for her, all chances
for happiness given up

to chemistry. Her only word was a helpless
yes when the doctor suggested fistfuls
of pills—pastels—that remind her of last summer's
clothes, fresh pressed, before her sweat
from the aroused sun inevitably crumpled them.

Devices for Torture

Because my words have become just whimpers
in some deserted primeval forest
with no safe tree or bird chirp,
silent like a prayer to some intemperate
spirit is the only way I know to say
goodbye. Finally today while you wander a new

continent, explore the intricate sameness
of palace and prison, filled with another
era's décolletage and well-crafted
devices for torture, I am left

dressed in spoiled red: the woman
who carries the ransacked basket—
no grandmother to please, no desire to
let the wolf in, ready to forget
the excitement of the terror
(did she really get torn, then eaten
by the imposter?—for now the end
escapes me). Cruelty knows

its goal, pain blooms
in the sorceress' hand and soon
I'll learn how to uncuff my wrists
in order to create the philter
that will make you plead for
what I will not give. When I live
and sing again, your ears
will ring discordant—all conversation
tossed to fire—and the scorched
path on which you rush
toward me will turn you to ash.

Heart, Kidney, Liver, Bone

Your photograph, the sachet filled
with shriveled flowers,
the silver ring, now lie
next to your letters in a container
the size that could hold
a heart, kidney, liver or bone.
You took those

from your friend when he died,
so others could have
the chance to dance on their own
axes as we once reeled
around the glow of the doting sun,
moved like protons and electrons,
turning planets into existence,
expanding as we spun our spirits
out to what we felt was divine.
Who now carries the gifts once inside

your friend the times he laughed
across the table from you?
How were you able to give them—
so matter of fact? And how dare
I question what you've done
for it's true others breathe
because of it. Yet
as I grasp this rectangular box,
for which I can find no right
place, it seems to be my body

that I clutch. O heart! mine
that it feels you try to thieve
while I'm still here and so alive.

Cremation

To burn your words out of my mind
I place them in the center of the red heat—
first the postcard from Hawaii that pretends
unending beach and immaculate sky.
The one that sends sweet wishes
signed with *Take Good Care*
as if in the blaze of this room
there's the possibility

you'd remember. Then your single poem
that amazed me—so good in its bad
taste. *Mouth, Lip, Tongue*
and all the rest of the body
parts—how you liked to
name them—curl then slip away
on what once was many textures
of paper. When only ash is left,
I question what I've done. Should I have

decorated the pyre with fall leaves,
fronted it with asters?
Will my spirit finally be free
of my flesh? Will I find the proper
niche to receive all of this?

To Lend Some Permanence

The plastic surgeon says the incision
would begin in the temple
hair in front of the ear,
then extend around the lobe
and back into the scalp.
With excessive skin cut out,
the underlying muscle and tissue
would be repositioned to
lend some permanence.
Then he hands me a mirror fancied
with gold plate and I glance
at myself, become every made-up hag
shopping the streets. This vanity

feels like love scratched
to base need—the plea
please stay O stay
forever. The terrible goodbyes

make the easy harder.
The neighbor's dog who rolled with his bone
disappeared from my noonday window
as did the child from up the block
who went to school and got shot.
I will not read the newspaper—
though the phone's still on the hook
and the calls arrive against
Cancer, Abuse, Suicide.
Save Us. Suddenly,

a small heart's available. Grief
and hope—two groups of families
gathered. While I wait
for the joy I remember
in your voice in bed
when we were new

and timeless. I give the doctor
back his monster
looking glass. I've seen enough
imperfection—loss—and now
just wish for a darkened room,
another chance for your lips to graze
my face, have the feeling it will last.

State of Being

I thought I was
beautiful until through your eyes
I saw it otherwise. True,
I asked, therefore I thought
I'd be able to handle
your reply. But it broke me so
I tried to change

your mind, have you
take it back, persuade
you with pufferies from other
loves—their *ooohs* and *aaahs,*
and I almost made you
believe what wasn't exactly

reality. Now I know
I used the question
to keep myself
away from you, for I was
tired, tired
of beauty—the unkind kind
that begs
the mirror to respond whole-
heartedly to *am I*
really ready? Today

I forget my skin, when
it glistened under you,
see only your slow coming down
upon me. The face's frightful
sag is a sight

on which we rarely focus
and if we do, never mention
unless we're willing to bend
over ourselves, study
our own reflections.

Enamel

At first I just caressed it—
as if caring for it—
then later, I wanted to break it
and wasn't deft enough.
So they used a tool
to smooth out the blade
I'd made of it, to adjust
my bite so I'd be unable

to fashion weapons
in my mouth when you didn't call
or when I'd tried to piece together
the old torn love
letters scattered on the floor
like the dust from the enamel
that was being filed.
The body's hardest substance

flaked over my wet face
and as I touched and brushed
off the most permanent part
of me, I thought of you—
all bones and flesh
wrapped around the wild
pain in my jaw—
and my fingers shook and couldn't stop
roiling the fallen grains.

Masochism

Gnarled hairs, one after another,
are enough to yank.
I don't require a hank
to feel my head a bruise
to pamper. Doctor, sometimes
I dream I snip
my nipples with manicuring
scissors. I let my husband use his
tongue to ruin each

thing I say to him,
while I pretend it doesn't matter.
You say I need a brain scan
to discover what is wrong
but I'd rather keep these thoughts
between me and my pen and paper—
though I permit my lovers to peek

inside and stay if they understand
the subtler methods of torture.
Who beat me so young in little
ways, Mother? Father?
I do not remember,
just that I always liked
to watch my skirt catch
fire, then douse it with
demitasse spoonfuls of water.

Obstruction

My envelope filled with notes
tears more as I add another scrap
of conversation—your voice rising
above the bad blood
count and the impotency caused
by drugs and/or the lack of "true" love—
as if after so much lying
with other women any bud
could push through and live. For over

a year my belly bloats and cramps—
an inner drool sours my soul—
while the doctor offers pills that seep
lethargy into me and weep me back
to bed. Naked and hungry,
like a hostage, I gobble
up deception and digest it
as hope. Cannot rid myself

of my small maps of where you
might show up—the hospital,
the widow's house, the home
of the woman whose husband
packed his bags and left,
cash in the drawer for you and her.
He doesn't care. Once, I called him
to find out where you were. He said "Boulder"
and I added it to my torn

pouch. Last week they x-rayed
my abdomen for an obstruction,
told me all paths were open
so there was nothing
to cut out, though the rupture
is always there when I double over
your spoiled words.

Between Rosh Hashanah and Yom Kippur

He opens The Book of Life and Death
where last year he penned in an uncle—
the world quieter for it—
and put me in the hospital
for nine days, my name
just lightly penciled on the page.
Tonight I call him in capitals—
Father, King—while still dialing

your number, not speaking.
The hush between us so humid
like the silent prayer
from the congregation—its anxious
words writhing in the air, steaming up:
Grant Me The Luck
Of Health And Wealth And Love
And I'll Be Good,
O Lord. Who hears the mute

clamor, the breaking of language
into the oblivion? Who can pull
the splinters out of the tongue
and attend to our quick
futures? What is really being
written here? Will we
talk closemouthed again next year?

March

The month the earth split slowly
into spring and the snowdrops
crept up through the patched
and muddied grass and bowed
their small white heads
as if to shed a human

tear, I wished you
luck and health and all
the good goodbye clichés—my anger
as hard as the hail
that smashed yesterday's windshields.
I don't understand this love—
the way old bulbs constantly
return the daffodils
from the insult of zero

degrees. The heat in your
voice forever swung
from red-hot to arctic
until in this season
my own speech froze
and what was planted
firm and long ago
had no reason to rise again.

Briefcase

I think about your eyes infatuated
with its smooth hide, how it glistened
and opened so easily in your hands,
how they glided over its outside,
inside—a fabric tough yet soft
like velvet—how well I parted
with it. Today you fill it with raised

hopes—contracts and prophylactics—
appear at my door holding
it. How straight the line
from your head to your wrist. A dignity

I lost the months you grabbed, then rushed
to distant places. I tried to stretch
my voice so far it broke, begging
into the phone *please come soon,*
I'm so alone. The hours
we made and missed connections collect

into a lump of time tiny enough
to wrap and bow.
How I want to watch you unsnap
the golden latch of that other gift,
and take this—malignant
or benign—to a spot I've never heard of
and where I never will arrive.

Bodily Fluids

When I chose not to open
my mouth, not to allow my tongue
its wild ride around the rim
of your smile and then into
your body's worn cave,
my speech grew thick
and indistinct so I gargled
with herbal oils until
when I saw you
I secreted an excess
I couldn't swallow
and a blockage to my midbrain
created a drool
that was my soul wandering
my throat and down
into the fatty sweat
that left a milky residue
and a memory of your
viscid sugar fluid;
my palms salted
and my blood flooded
with oxygen, became the brightest red,
because I knew
all we could share
was the inhale of air.

Itch

after being bitten by a flea

The bites I scratched to fluid
red scar my legs.
The others that swelled large
hemorrhages—quarters of blood
that flooded my shins—
have vanished
with no blemish left of the throb
of wanting to dig into the bottomless

itch. The metamorphosis of the flea
from harmless egg to adult
and its hunt for a host
remind me of us. How I craved

the inflammation—the fierce dream
of the piercing. I can count the times
I ripped down past the surface
of myself. Each remains a blot
I can't bleach out,
while when I never touch
the heated mound, the spot
lies flat and quiet—gone.

Ninth-Month Rhythms

The pageant of blood soon to finish,
the most that's left is a couple of years
of trickle then gush, trickle
then stop. In the mirror she plucks
gray snarls from harmonious brown
strands, her busy hands moving
down to rest on the mound once
rich with rough curls, now thinned
to a stingy silhouette.
She wonders will she be left

with just baldness, nothing
for a lover to strum through.
Where will the rhythms come from,

what will she give birth to?
In the ninth and final month her body
always knew how to meter itself,
her breasts emerging like white violets—
reflexed stars. Now they fall
and her spine, the lovely stem
of her that held each blossoming child proud,
begins to bend. In her moist bed

she awakens to her own
coo and groan, caressing
old images of herself in full bloom.

Jowls

Now it's my turn to become
the old woman, slowly
as this planet drags
away from the sun and the air cools
my body down—my limbs
sometimes bend like twigs bowed
from the onslaught of snow.
I learn how easy it is to sleep

with the TV on, lulled by
a commentator's description
of a missile's plunge,
or to linger at my magnifying mirror
as I finger my skin,
try to resculpt the roundness
that is being undone. No one

notices yet, their eyes not as large
as my looking
glass that so assuredly predicts
collapse. The world
releases us so fast. I've watched
those who plead for a few more
minutes—the hope for
one last passionate kiss.
And I still check to see

if you are there,
but have stopped waiting for a voice—
just the click
of your picking up is enough.
Then I let the receiver drop.

Cathedral

I'm not sacred anymore, now filled
with rifled openings
where hope once grew young in
every mouth with simple one-syllable
words like trust and bliss.
The years have left my lips

silenced in prayer or pain
while ruffians and surgeons,
both with no time
for love or grace, construct
my body into arch and slope
and will not look into my face.

Hysterectomy as Metaphor

Nothing has been literally
lost, just a suggestion of sentences
strung in old familiar
jargon like *When*
your father comes home
he'll clean out
your mouth (his lubricated fist
depressing my tongue,
fingers spreading down
as if he were going to rip out
my uvula and what seemed like
the sweet juice of freedom
siphoned—the words, the "dirty"
words, supposedly being
shut up). I wanted to scream

at all of them. Men unable
to carry anyone's destiny
in the ripe pear shape examined
me over and over as I turned
my eyes to the cold
thin walls, my torn
paper gown becoming privacy's poor
joke like someone's
I'll love you forever as long
as I can come inside.
Here where it's still warm

I've locked the door
and glided into bed
with only my hands holding me—
like a perfect seed—a little
girl, all amazing possibility.

Menopause

Her ovaries dry as asters
in the October wind
would not yield an egg
and she believed the poems
needed one for even
a first word to come.
She felt the pen
had nothing to bleed
through its still straight stem
and all she did was draw on
the yellow paper, as if begging
like she had to her last
lost lover to come back,
and he did only to leave her
paler and more parched,
so that when she spoke
she'd moisten her lips
after each phrase.
Then she bought a pencil
thinking an eraser

could take away the winter
that was upon her,
ease her through spring into summer
when everything flowed
best, the world gushing
flowers. But her body
had lost its seasons and time
became a straight line
and the pad stayed blank,
waiting while she paused—
planted and dormant.

Indian Summer

I cool, then rise to the heat
again, to the candlelit sun
as it flames the oak blood
red and the sugar maple
yellow to scarlet.

The wind becomes an anxious breeze
begging me to let it in,
to please stay young,
and I say *Yes*—a promise
to this October afternoon
as if it were and will be forever
my constant, fevered, only lover.

Oral Interpretation

I'm starting over with one breath,
a sigh, the sound *fffffffff*—
head down, shoulders dropped,
feet a body width apart,
knees unsteadily holding
the half squat. This is how
the shaping begins

to erase the early whine,
the weary twang,
to find the path to the husky
Yes, so when the longed-for
moment comes, my tongue will
be ready with the lush and lilting
answer. Standing erect

I'm practicing *mmmmmmmmmm*
on the exhale now,
feeling the vibrations on my lips,
changing pitch with a *hummmmmmmmah*
flying up from my chest.
I haven't gotten deep enough
for words yet,
and if I talk you'll recognize
the old stubborn child noise—
that constant thrashing

against the palate
as if it were every bolted door.
Someday you'll hear me, free.
Touching you, my voice
will be exactly what I say.

Mania

Sometimes I talk too much
at a shrill pitch and the bitch
part of me carries off
my conversation in directions
I'd never travel with more peaceful
lips. But when my brain swells
and pushes on the small bones
of my face, what spills out
seems so rich. I think
everyone loves me so much.
Until, alone with the bloated
moon, I hear the rattle
of my voice and its twist—
the gnarled path it takes running
after any catch, grabbing
first place in a race
it does not want to enter,
accepting the trophy
with a curtsy practiced
for royalty. Hater of both halves
of myself—raving
slave, desperate dictator.

Nerve

If I could catapult myself into the air,
float through the blue with the ease of a bird,
then I would leave, not be left
alone these many years with the fear
of being blown to bits among the stars.
Yet, I know for each of us it can only come
to this. Anyway I look at it,
it's always the same nerve

being pinched. My leg rarely feels the calm
of the ground, even when I slip my feet into
their wedged supportive shoes, carefully
constructed to minimize the ache,
so how can I expect to take
the leap into the sky? *Goodbye*

I softly say to you, *Godbless,*
and while I pray in my chair, stare
at the children playing catch across the street,
or decide to lie on my back
with pillows bunched underneath—
like a corpse rich with false
peace—you'll be up there closer
to the power of the moon.
And when you finally drift down, kiss
me, you'll talk about where you've gone,
run your hand along my hip,
traveling the small distance
of my outer limit until I moan
stop, I'm too frightened of the pain of going on.

How High

Each time after it's over
I ask him how high
we flew (in this single engine
jalopy plane that hammers harder
than my heart on its most desperate
days) and he says so far
1,000 to 2,000 feet. Hardly near
any star except I
did leave earth after
so many years I won't tell. A secret

like my grandmother's age.
Yesterday I passed over her,
restless in her grave,
surrounded by air truly sky
blue, and as I did, didn't I see
my grandfather wave,
or is he higher, with the jets
or beyond? When we took off
my husband—so bent in the back
he could barely touch my neck—
yelled *You're doing it*
and I whispered *yes*
like the first time love
merged with sex. I forgot

about the man who tempted me
to the ground and how I couldn't
have guessed he was the angel
of death. And all of this is part
of that. I had to wrench
myself away so I came up here
for $42.00 on the half hour—
to rise and dip,
lose my breath and get it back
and ask how high I need to go
to regain all of my soul.

Leaving

Beyond my grandmother finally
in the grave, her mouth
at rest, her desperate
words pressed six feet under,
with only syllables left
in my head that still can flail
inside my skull—beyond the cradle
of my tongue in some unfamiliar mouth,
its reckless fling at small freedoms,
I am leaving, hungry
to follow the plump moon,
to be higher than anyone's
screams can make me jump
or passionate embrace can
lift me. I surrender

all my amulets—the waxy
green strings from Life Savers
that I twist at funerals, the tarnished
ring I lose and find, given
by a man whose smile belies
his heart's ruin. My mind

has left so many times
in my dreams—the plane heightens
but never lands.
Doctor, what does it mean?
is what I'd run around and ask.
I'd see my family before me,
black-and-white old photographs,
their lineup
of warnings. *Do not*
touch the phone, icebox,
yourself. I'd rub
their voices out with all kinds
of astringent soaps, my body
dried to oven-cracked—no
lotion ever proved to be the balm—
while I kept looking
for the antidote. My suitcase is

almost empty now—only room
for soft sweater and slacks, pretty
bra, underpants, blusher
for when I pale at
take-off, deodorant to quiet
the arousal of rising above
my chair by the window,
lipstick for after love, after a meal.

Half Price

Your poems have so much sex in them
she mutters and when I tell
her they're not about sex, but despair
and death, she changes
the subject—talks about the coat
she just purchased
for half price and I am left
speechless. Once, she was my only word

and I'm sure she must have smiled
on me, made me feel like *good
little girl.* But now in this maze
of sentences I do more than hold on to
the regimented hug and kiss,
am willing to experiment
with the lick and bite. I know

how to hide my anguish
when we talk, use all the clichés:
*how are you I am fine
I know the weather's lousy
today tomorrow forever.*
It's only with my pen we pay
the price and I'm reduced
to the child who won't behave
and isn't very nice.

Suicide

Depression's thin-skinned daughter,
awake in her own deep grave
of disordered sleep, frozen
by the burning terror of having
wandered too far nether,
listens to mother
tell how it is

under the stone, locked in the vault,
her face eternally pressed
like a lily in a book—
how obsessed she was with death—
and now she says since
she's her

mimicker, and better,
Superstar, the girl
must come to visit
more often, to please
consider not leaving
so fast, stay past
the expanse and spin of worlds
she can't control
and the child answers *yes*.

Calendar

I begin the page with pencil
as January freezes fragile
icicles outside my window, breakable
like the thin lead
that records where I'll go
and easily allows me
to change my mind
so what was promised,
then taken back—erased—will not be
found. The future as yet
unknown, with no excuses, remains
fresh—smooth like the first snow
of the new year before the mailman's
shoes ruin it. Soon enough

my calendar's innocent untouched
months will be filled and emptied.
I used to use ink to chronicle
the hours where I'd be,
confident that I'd arrive.
But now, with something less
permanent, my commitment to the days
fades more easily.

Susan Hahn

In the ambulance between the quick
decisions made on the two-way
radio and the moans of the man inches
from the muddied floor, whose clothes
the paramedics tore off,
they kept asking me who I was,
could I spell my name and
over and over I'd tell them
susan hahn s-u-s-a-n-h-a-h-n.
It sounded wrong—
too bland, too short
with all those double s's, a's, h's, n's.
A drab white kept coming
to mind like a rag,
a too easily grabbed
burial cloth. I wanted more

letters as if that would hold me
to the solid world I'd just left
before the smack and spin from the other
car—that driver's desperate rush
to take his doubled-up passenger
to the hospital and how now
I was going too. I'm not ready

to know what happened to the man
they harnessed to the steel board—
his sleepy eyes slowly rolling off
course as the men who worked on him
shouted *What's Your Name.*
Only once did he say it as we sped
to Emergency. When they carried him away
I whispered in a scratched voice
something I can't quite remember
and which he probably didn't
hear, like *take care, be fine
please,* his name, then mine.

Incontinence

When love gushed out
of me too cloudy—
not the amber
it should be—
and I couldn't control
my permeability or the journey

of my capillaries,
I grew heavy
with liquid, gravid
with disease of the nut-
shaped gland lodged within
my twists of brain.
I wanted to run

backwards through ontogeny,
far from dry
land, for I couldn't
concentrate or conserve
my wits or salts.
The sea seemed

the only safe place
to let go
and live again—
a return to where
it all began, before
the urgency and burn
of anything human.

The Hope

Sometimes when rocking off to longed-for
sleep—death's sweet dress
rehearsal—I feel you
deep inside me and hear
my words *harder, harder,*
as if they'll awake me more
alive. That's the dream
of you I keep
for the moment when I die:
the hope that then
you'll discover me again.

The Hemlock Society

May 5

Because the "how to" book
has not arrived,
I'm still here, my life a noose
my neck cannot unloosen—
if I move it to the left
or to the right you are still nowhere
in sight and the sounds of you
are just my own. Today,
you moved and unlisted your phone—
the path ends quick and quiet.
I've put out a tablespoon

but as yet don't know the mix
that will do the trick—
lift me off the hook of this
life and let me go into the silence
that is now your voice.

May 12

I chose the clear bag
so I could see
the fossil ginkgo tree
that comes slowly back
to life each May,
and didn't pick the suggested
rubberbands, but the velvet ribbon—
the fire red—that divided
my hair the time in bed
I begged for *more*. Death was
distant that day that evolved
into eternity. Now I blend

the powders with my favorite pudding
and bless the young gods—
Seconal, Tuinal, and Nembutal—
leave out the One
from Sunday school,
knowing He would not be
pleased with me. Love

has leveled my body,
broken the fine bones
of my soul—it will not float up.
My plastic sack is ready.
I wear it like a hat.

Heart

Her sick heart is snap frozen
and sent across the city.
Soon researchers will wash
themselves in their sterile rooms,
ready to step into immaculate
gowns. Her buried body

has no use for it and those
who dissect it will never find
what interrupted its perfect beat.
That part is caught elsewhere
in the unknown, like the mystery
of why she bound herself

to the phone, dialed his number
over and over. How flushed
she was against the flat rings,
and when he finally answered—
out of breath from the rush
of someone else's touch—
there was nothing left
for him to give into
the receiver, and her heart
lost the rhythm it possessed
before she ever knew his voice.
Now it thaws

in the laboratory
as if it will share
its secret, and a pathologist
cuts into it—eager,
like a lover whose dream has died
and who keeps looking
for what killed it.

The Soul's Aerial View of the Burial

Everything is black or white—
the mourners' heavy wool coats
wander over the crisp snow,
their arms holding onto whoever's left—
while I wait for them to seal
the perfect rectangular hole
so I can go—to where
I do not know.
But for now I muse above the bony
trees, about how fragile
the dance is that they do,
and how I don't remember
ever having such an unfettered view.